Musings from Beneath the Butterfly Tree

Maisie Chambers

BookLeaf Publishing

India | USA | UK

Presentation by *BookLeaf Publishing*

Web: www.bookleafpub.com

E-mail: info@bookleafpub.com

ISBN: 9789360943516

First edition 2024

To Mama Bear and Dad,

For everything.

*And my brother William, for not much at all
(though I love you regardless)*

ACKNOWLEDGEMENT

I'd like to thank all my best friends from school-Kirsty, Sienna, Sara, Nat- for putting up with my ridiculous poems throughout sixth form. Your bemused smiles are what helped me write a great many of these ones.

Thank you also to the newest of best friends, Rowan. You taught me that love can be found where you least anticipate it, and when you're most in need of it.

Last, but certainly not least, I'd like to thank my wonderful cat, aptly named Lucifer. Most of these poems were written with her curled up on my chest, and I couldn't have asked for a better editor.

PREFACE

As a poet (with the loosest application of the term possible) who began writing at only eight or nine, my works have spanned a great variety of topics, from fishfinger weddings to dogs running along the beach.

While I can't guarantee the same fluctuation in subject that comes with years of development between pieces, these twenty one poems- written in twenty one days- aren't exactly confined to a single genre. There is no motif that runs through them all for eagle-eyed readers to pick up on. If, by chance, this book ever finds its way into the hands of a student, and is required reading... don't believe a word of what your professor says about it. The only thing connecting these poems is their author, who happens to be an emotionally turbulent teenage girl.

Got it? Then let's begin.

The Seagulls' Plight

When wind whips through the upright grass
And renders it fit to pray
I find myself at the cliff side
Watching seagulls take off at the bay

They march onwards to their runways
Their calls lost in the breeze
And when they stretch triumphant wings
Their goal seems almost to tease

One by one, they flap, and rise
Into the boundless sky
And as the wind comes rolling in
They're tossed about like die

Yet even when they're teetering
At the mercy of the thermals
Their wingbeats are unwavering
Their resilience eternal

Some days I see stupidity
In their wars waged on the gale
I laugh at their continual march
To a task that's doomed to fail

On others, though, I understand
Why they beat their wings in vain
Of course, with nothing ventured
There's nothing left to gain

At last, they'll reach the shoreline
Bow their heads into the foam
And as they announce their victory
I make my way back home

I often think of the seagulls
And as humans, we share in their plight
Though the wind often offers us no reprieve
What else can we do but take flight?

On the future

A crisp bag floats down outside Poundland
Like a leaf just released from a tree
I wonder when it became normal
For plastic to be all we see

I wonder if in half a century
If the whole planet's not dead
They'll fashion more leaves from old PVC
Make them fall from glass towers instead.

A Visit to a Friend

We eat Clementines sat in your kitchen
It's the first time in days I've felt hope
The smell of citrus and the sinking sun
Makes me think of The Orange by Cope

In the night, you snore like a foghorn
And the dogs outside bark at the moon
I smile at the way your blanket
Seems to swaddle you like a cocoon

The next morning we walk to the station
You hug me and smile from the gate
Last week, I thought about ending things
But today, I think I might wait.

The Donkey that used to be Gifted: a Poem about Burnout

There once lived a man with a donkey
He paraded the creature 'round town
Swore on its fitness with God as his witness
And constantly weighed the beast down.

He didn't care if its legs shook
It could walk, and that was enough
With every stop to a newly stocked shop
The donkey was packed with more stuff

At last, its trembling knees buckled
And all that it carried was shattered
The man grew incensed, and spoke great offence
His own reputation was tattered

The donkey's old feats were soon scoffed at
Despite all the weights it had borne
Now it was a mule fit for pure ridicule
Much less than the carts it had drawn

Nobody cared for its welfare
Now exhausted, the ass had no use

But to feel it had failed, and lower its tail
And think it deserved the abuse

The man soon paraded new beasts
Each one doomed to an end like the last
One wrong step in the test, it failed like the rest
Its time of firm praise quickly passed

There's no doubt of the source of the problem
The weight was too much to be lifted
But it's easy to blame, and confer all the shame
To the donkey who used to be 'gifted'.

An Ode to Icarus

When wax wings started to dampen
The roots of each quill turning brown
Do you think Icarus became frightened
At the thought of his plummeting down?

Did he watch the quickening melting
With nostrils flaring from terror
Did he see the droplets careen down his legs
And realise the depth of his error?

Did he think perhaps he could fight it
Reverse what the Gods put in place
Did he beat his wings more ferociously
Kick his legs to keep up the pace?

Do you think he felt the wax sloughing
Off his shoulders and back like burnt skin
If he did, what made him keep going?
Did he still really think he might win?

Or did everything else fade from view
In his journey towards something higher
Perhaps he carried on, unawares
That the best thing would be to retire

And then when the wax came a-dripping
Did he think it was nothing but sweat?
Did he wipe his brow and tell himself
That he had a good while to go yet?

He didn't notice the difference in weight
Til his stomach dropped with the fall
Only then, did Daedalus' words
Come to his memory at all

He'd vowed to heed the stern warning
When his feet were still planted on ground
But it's hard to remember you're fallible
When brightness is all that's around

It's only when wings melt completely
That we realise we're destined to burn
From earth, we're labelled invincible
But always to earth we'll return.

And on that pitiful tumbling down
At last we know what we've done
Just like frightened young Icarus
Who flew too close to the sun.

The Hoodie

The other day while in the shops
I found something quite strange
An odd new piece of clothing
Part of Primark's lounge wear range

It consisted of two hoodies
But fused into one item
Two hoods, two arms, and stretched out wide
I still was unenlightened

Only when I ventured close
Could I discern its use
And at that realisation
A softened smile slipped loose

The thing was meant for lovers
Who wish to share the space
By keeping warm and keeping in
The other's soft embrace

To some, it seems ridiculous
A claustrophobic hell
And maybe Primark just needed
Another thing to sell

Still, there's something beautiful
In loving one so much
You'd buy a conjoined hoodie
Just to stay within their touch.

The Raincloud

Today I woke up with a raincloud
Perching right over my head
I told it to move, but it refused
So I curled up inside of my bed

I knew that soon it would thunder
My prediction turned out to be true
I felt the rumblings in my chest
Breathed quick til my lips coloured blue

The raindrops came skittering down my cheeks
And I hugged my knees to my chest
I prayed the weather report would show
My storm was moving west

But some storms are persistent
Some rainclouds are stubborn, you see
And the one hovering above my head
Was committed to bothering me

It chilled with every last droplet
And each thunderbolt made my hands shake
I laid back against my soaked pillows
And cursed that I was awake

The longer the raincloud stayed put there
The more that I started to doubt
If ever a day had been sunny and dry
Before my raincloud came about

I couldn't recall when I'd last walked around
With only blue skies overhead
I didn't know how I had ever been able
To pull myself out of my bed

When I speak to others about it
This cloud that won't leave me alone
They tell me theirs went, with a little time spent
Getting out of the house on their own

It's just a light shower, they say
A positive outlook's essential
But their rainclouds seem more like drizzle
And mine is quite close to torrential

The truth, I find, is a sad one
That not all of our storms are made equal
Some live their lives with just one to weather
While for others, there's always a sequel

For some people, sunny is normal
They rarely go out with a coat
But for me, the best is a rainbow
Enough colour to keep me afloat

One day, I hope to see sunshine
No forecaster calling for rain
Today is not such a fortunate day
Come tomorrow, I'll try again.

Post-it notes

There's a collection of post-its I keep on my wall
A list of the things I must do
'Watch fifty sunsets' and 'have my first kiss'
Reasons to keep pushing through

I used to think my life would end
When I pulled down the last post-it note
But now, I simply write new ones
More tasks and more time to devote

One day perhaps, my ideas will run dry
And I'll have nothing else left to give
But for now, I have so many post-its to stick
And a great many lives left to live.

Electrical Friend

Electrical friend at the end of my phone
So much more than these pixels on screen
Thanks to your presence, I'm never alone
And at last I am finally seen

There are times where I scorn the refinement
Of this world in the palm of my hand
An ironic bionic confinement
Just one grain on a beach full of sand

But then all this electrical chatter
Connects me to someone like you
Walls between worlds start to shatter
The gentlest hand reaches through

"It's okay", you say, "I am here now"
The voice message flows like the tide
In uncertain times, a sure little vow
And at once, the world's not so wide

Electrical friend at the end of the wire
I love you, and I won't deny it
Let the satellites fall and be swallowed by fire
Still my side of the line won't go quiet.

An Ode to Luci

There is no love purer than that of my cat
When she enters my room, tail curled high
She has all of the bed to lay down upon
Yet it's under my chin she must lie.

She's done so since she was a baby
And that same tiny size she's remained
I wonder if God offered growth if she chose
But to keep her claimed spot, she abstained.

Marbles

17

Sometimes, at night in my bedroom,
I worry life's passing me by
That my time on this earth is a snapshot
Just one lash in the blink of an eye

I watch all my friends move away from here
Scattered like marbles on floor
They roll into the dust beneath my old sofa
And I'm told it's best I find more

But what if it's not what I'm meant for
This quick jump to one thing from the last
What if I'm doomed to search evermore
For marbles I lost in the past?

By Choice

I don't think I could ever forget you
Nor find any reason to get through
If by rotten chance, I'd not met you
That one day when my world fell apart

You yanked me right up from the rubble
Brushed me off, told me it was no trouble
Brought me all of my love back in double
And mended my shattered old heart

I'm not sure I can ever repay you
For showing me there was a way to
Love completely despite what life may do
To strip you of self-worth and voice

But what I can do is endeavour
To show you, no matter the weather
We'll face life's rough climate together
I love you. I do so by choice.

New Year, Old Habits

On TV, I watch the crowds in NYC
Gather to watch the ball drop
A haughty flock of black-tie bourgeoisie
Reminding us they're still on top

That despite the destruction they've wrought
here
In the endless pursuit of more wealth
They're happy to crack open another beer
And drink to their own cracking health

In this moment, the stars above glisten
And Times Square's bedazzled in light
What need have these people to listen
To any old sad poor soul's plight?

To them, this new year is beginning
New business, new suits, new vacations
So long as the world keeps on spinning
There'll be more human rights violations

At last, the ball starts descending
Impaling itself on the city
It's the great, spectacular ending
And in New York, there's no time for pity.

Up in that boundless night, fireworks skim
And Times square erupts into cheer
That old ball hangs limply, its lights flicker dim
Is it really a happy new year?

Peru

One day in the near future
When all my plans fall through
We'll climb aboard a rowing boat
And sail to Peru

The navy ships'll pass us by
And honk their mighty horns
We'll watch a thousand sunsets
And endure a hundred storms

My family will miss me
But most people won't mind
If I sail away with you, my dear
And leave my old life behind.

God and Man

Men wage wars over money
To violence they pledge their devotion
And yet, a woman in power is funny
Because *she'd* be led by emotion

My mother gave my brother life
Later, I built his bed
And yet, when women's creation is rife
God is a man instead?

Parakeet

"What bird would you be?", my friend asked me
"If you had to be one at all"
I pondered canaries in little brass cages
The pigeons that perched on my wall.
I can't recall what I told her
Maybe a starling or wren
But now, I'd have a new answer
To give her if she asked again.
I only realised days later
When I chose to look up from my feet
And observed in a tree that shook in the breeze
The green wings of a young parakeet
Once I had taken a moment
To watch her preen and ruffle above
I knew I had more in common with her
Than any old pigeon or dove
Each time when I watch her kind flocking
It strikes me as truly bizarre
That such a queer creature's a regular feature
In England and not in Qatar
Just like her, I'm not suited
To this cold little isle that I've grown from
If I had her wings, I'd gather my things
And England would quickly be flown from
Yet just like her, I remain here

With the grey and the wind and the rain
As my bright green feathers are muddied
And my tropical dreams start to wane
At the end of the day, we're no kin, though
And this Summer, I'm migrating west
I take back Parakeet, I'm a swallow
This old broken country's no nest.

Stammer

They say the eyes are windows
To the soul that lies beneath
In that case, the mouth's a door
A passageway marked by teeth

For most, this door is open
The words flow through unpersuaded
So what a shock it was to me
When I found my door barricaded

A stammer had rendered me speechless
And while my mind remained quick
My lips could not voice the thoughts within
Letters disappeared brick by brick

First to go were words starting with 'o'
Of octopus, orange, and oat
I pushed and pushed to force the words out
But still they stayed lodged in my throat

'A' was quick to follow the pattern
And 'and' became evil to me
Then 'e', my vowels were turning to ash
Each one a newfound enemy

When 'i' and 'u' went tumbling down too
My confidence shattered like glass
For a time, not a single hand was raised
To contribute answers in class

I knew that if I opened my mouth
My attempts could only be bleak
I resigned myself to live without
That primal need to speak

But it isn't such a simple thing
To commit yourself to silence
I am no humble Nepalese monk
Without my words came violence

I grew frustrated with every day
That passed with lips kept sealed
Til one morning, I gave up the ghost
And forced my cruel stammer to yield

It took many weeks spent abattle
To force the beast to submission
But at last, I set down my sword
For I had accomplished my mission

So, take that, you devilish vowels
Your plan for my silence fell through
Orange and octopus, and and away
Fuck u, and fuck and e and i too.

Girlhood

Girlhood is braids made on school fields
And necklaces weaved out of grass
It's staring daggers at the man in the club
Who dared to touch your friend's ass
It's holding ladybirds in the garden
Stopping boys from stepping on snails
It's pinching cheeks and refused desserts
And evenings spent standing on scales.

Girlhood is late night discussions
Muffled giggles when you're meant to be
sleeping
It's travelling to public toilets in packs
To make sure that no Toms are peeping
It's folding up paper for fortune tellers
And making the things pop with colour
It's watching how cat calls erase a friend's smile
And make her complexion grow duller.

Girlhood is playing at families
Holding dolls with the greatest of caution
It's watching the news with a tightness of chest
When another state outlaws abortion
It's code words made up for crushes
And confessions that leave mouths agape

It's the furious tears when the judge decides
That the man isn't guilty of rape.

Girlhood is making a dance with your friends
And forcing your mothers to watch it
It's being talked over in a subject you know
By arrogant guys that will botch it
It's holding hands with a girl you just met
Announcing you'll be friends for life
It's rejecting connecting your worth to a man
Being more than a 'sister' or 'wife'.

Girlhood is fighting with all that we've got
To live without fear or shame
Girlhood is loving, and living to say
"We're girls, we're women

Say our names."

This winter, it's snowing in Gaza

This winter, it's snowing in Gaza
Great white flakes set adrift in the air
They fall from the ceilings with every new blast
And move those inside to speak prayer

There aren't any lights strung on houses
For there aren't any homes to adorn
Instead, there are candles, to huddle around
And to light for the loved ones they mourn

Back in England, the shops are all bustling
We live in our own little bubble
Humming to Carey and digging for gifts
While in Gaza, they're digging through rubble

I know that this fight isn't over
There's much more to be done for them yet
But this winter, it's snowing in Gaza
And for their sake I'll never forget.

The music of home

The beating drum of constant dart hits
A clatter on floors with oft missed targets
Victorious roars when the ball's in the net
Or frustrated groans and remarks of regret
Snoring when Dad falls asleep at midday
The scratching of claws in the cat's litter tray
Wind groaning under the doors late at night
The constant hum-buzz of the old kitchen light
Toilet flush and the rush of the tap in the bath
The crackle of footsteps that tread our path
Howls of distrust from the dog standing fast
Nose raised to alert anyone walking past

Oh how I will miss, when abroad I must roam
The incongruous symphony of this old home.

Musings from beneath the butterfly tree

On Summer days I'd run about
And chase the butterflies
Unfettered by the creeping doubt
That soon would cloud my skies

I watched them in their dancing
Circling the purple flowers
Til moonlight came advancing
And they fled for farther bowers

I used to walk on silent springs
To catch a glimpse so fleeting
Of patterns swirling on the wings
Seen only when not beating

The twitching of a single limb
Would send these wings aflutter
I fought hard against every whim
Suppressed each breath and mutter

And once in prime position
I saw creatures in repose
Their natural disposition
Being thus, to perch and doze

While my heart did leap to see
Them dance a vibrant number
Beneath that old butterfly tree
I loved to watch their slumber

As children, we are born to dance
And never stop our spinning
Sucked into a dizzy trance
Til ruddy-faced and grinning

In watching this beautiful fleet
Adjourn their dance to drowse
I learned that it is something sweet
That observance allows

And yes, it is no simple thing
To find the time to ponder
How the wren unfurls her wing,
The leaves that fall beyond her

But sometimes, on those moonlit nights
The evenings of December
I shift my gaze from the last lights
Evinced by burning ember

I see her standing just as tall
Her branches stretched out free
That same old friend when I was small

My proud butterfly tree

At last, when winter shucks her coat
And sweet springtime soon sings
I'll sit right there, and time devote
To watching patterned wings.